Dear Parents,

Welcome to the Scholastic Reader series. We have taken over 80 years of experience with teachers, parents, and children and put it into a program that is designed to match your child's interests and skills.

Level 1—Short sentences and stories made up of words kids can sound out using their phonics skills and words that are important to remember.

Level 2—Longer sentences and stories with words kids need to know and new "big" words that they will want to know.

Level 3—From sentences to paragraphs to longer stories, these books have large "chunks" of texts and are made up of a rich vocabulary.

Level 4—First chapter books with more words and fewer pictures.

It is important that children learn to read well enough to succeed in school and beyond. Here are ideas for reading this book with your child:

• Look at the book together. Encourage your child to read the title and make a prediction about the story.
• Read the book together. Encourage your child to sound out words when appropriate. When your child struggles, you can help by providing the word.
• Encourage your child to retell the story. This is a great way to check for comprehension.
• Have your child take the fluency test on the last page to check progress.

Scholastic Readers are designed to support your child's efforts to learn how to read at every age and every stage. Enjoy helping your child learn to read and love to read.

—**Francie Alexander**
Chief Education Officer
Scholastic Education

For Andrew, Bryan,
and Matthew McNamara,
with thanks to Dave
— J.M.

To Abigail Dodge
— W.W.

Text copyright © 2006 by Jean Marzollo.
"Chain Reaction" from *I Spy Mystery* © 1993 by Walter Wick; "Flight of Fancy";
"Blast Off"; "Sweet Dreams"; and "Ballerina" from *I Spy Fantasy* © 1994 by
Walter Wick; "Be My Valentine" and "Sorting and Classifying" from *I Spy School Days*
© 1995 by Walter Wick; "Full Moon at Dawn," "Good Morning," and "The Empty Hall"
from *I Spy Spooky Night* © 1996 by Walter Wick.

Library of Congress Cataloging-in-Publication Data is available.

ISBN 0-439-73865-2

10 9 8 7 6 5 4 3   06 07 08 09 10
Printed in the U.S.A.   23
First printing, March 2006

I SPY
A BUTTERFLY

Riddles by Jean Marzollo
Photographs by Walter Wick

Scholastic Reader — Level 1

SCHOLASTIC INC.

New York Toronto London Auckland Sydney
Mexico City New Delhi Hong Kong Buenos Aires

I spy

a butterfly,

 a silver jack,

a fish,

 a mask,

and a yellow tack.

I spy

a deer,

 a little blue sail,

a window frog,

and an elephant's tail.

I spy

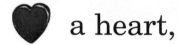 a heart,

a lightbulb,

 a spoon,

and two men ready

for a trip to the moon.

I spy

 two E's,

a red-and-yellow star,

 a hot dog,

a lion,

 and a star on a car.

I spy

a yo-yo,

 a crayon,

a duck,

 a blue kangaroo,

and a small cement truck.

I spy

a paper clip,

a plaid bow tie,

two fans,

a cage,

and a butterfly.

I spy

sunglasses,

 a wooden guitar,

a deer,

 three crayons,

and a little red car.

I spy

a ghost,

a fork,

a bat,

and a dark green face

 Boo

with a bright yellow hat.

I spy

a carriage,

 a sea horse,

a clock,

 two frying pans,

a snake,

 and a lock.

I spy

 a spoon,

a clear glass whale,

 a pair of pliers,

and a shadow cat's tail.

I spy two matching words.

elephant's tail

 shadow cat's tail

clock

I spy two matching words.

bright yellow hat

heart

red-and-yellow star

I spy two words that start
with the letter F.

fork

two fans

crayon

I spy two words that start with the letter W.

 wooden guitar

mask

 clear glass whale

I spy two words that end with the letter G.

hot dog

 lion

window frog

I spy two words that end with the letter E.

 snake

cage

 bat

I spy two words that rhyme.

 spoon

 moon

 sea horse

I spy two words that rhyme.

 bow tie

 kangaroo

butterfly

Collect all the I Spy Readers!

 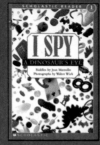 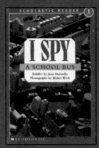 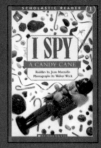

 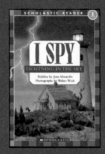 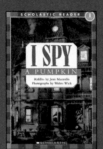 

And the original I Spy books, too!

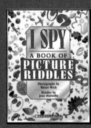  

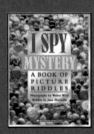  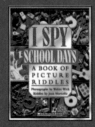 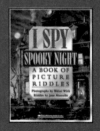 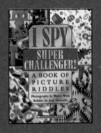

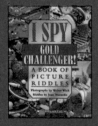 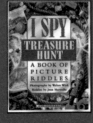  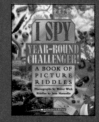